Sagittarius Predictions and Rituals 2024

Astrologers

Alina A. Rubi and Angeline Rubi

Published Independently

Astrologers: Alina A. Rubi and Angeline Rubi

Email: rubiediciones29@gmail.com

Editing: Angeline A. Rubi

rubiediciones29@gmail.com

Who is Sagittarius?

Dates: November 23 - December 21

Day: Thursday

Color: purple blue, green and white

Element: fire

Compatibility: Libra, Gemini, Leo, and Aries

Symbol: ♐

Mode: mutable

Polarity: male

Ruling Planet: Jupiter

House: 9

Metal: Tin

Quartz: Turquoise and Topaz

Constellation: Sagittarius

Sagittarius Personality

Sagittarius is one of the most positive signs of the zodiac. They are versatile and love adventure and the unknown. They are open-minded to new ideas and experiences and maintain an optimistic attitude even when the going gets tough.

They are open and cheerful people who transmit positive energy to the people around them. They have a religious and spiritual nature and high morals.

Sagittarius is a sign that loves to discover, travel abroad, explore, adventure, risk, try their luck, broaden their knowledge, and enjoys their social life. Sagittarius takes life with humor, with philosophy.

They are attracted to risky sports and those that can be practiced alone because of their strong self-confidence, travel that allows them to meet cultures and religions other than their own, nature, knowledge, religion, philosophy, laws, justice, and social norms.

If they enjoy a stable and balanced relationship, Sagittarians show their best side and will be excellent fathers and husbands, transmitting moral and ethical values to their children, besides showing their jovial, cheerful, and enthusiastic side among their own. They are very passionate and carpe diem could be their motto in life since they are so enthusiastic that they do not want to waste any second of their days. They are good friends, noble, loyal, and sincere. Precisely this sincerity can turn against them and create conflicts with people who think differently from them.

They are empathetic, good counselors, they are positive, they tend to simplify things, they see the good side of everything and therefore tend to self-deception. They do not like routine, they are dynamic, adaptable, honest, and naive. Their audacity makes them like nature, travel, adventure.

A Sagittarius is a spiritual, philosophical, and deep soul. One of the things that is most appealing about Sagittarians is their ability to see the bigger picture, and to be able to give advice for their friends' problems. Sagittarians attract wealth or generate it. They have the ideas, energy, and talent to make their vision a reality. However, wealth alone is not enough.

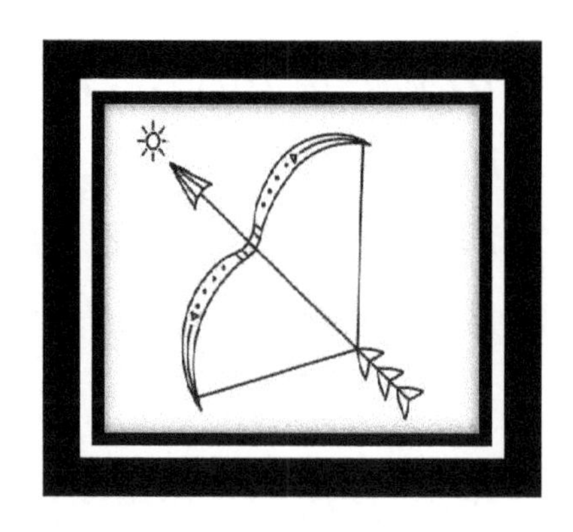

General Horoscope for Sagittarius

This will be a promising year for Sagittarius. Your personal and professional life will be good, although they will have their share of challenges and responsibilities.

You will have to make some important decisions; therefore, you should rely on the advice of your friends and loved ones.

This is a period that will take you out of your routine and encourage you to pursue your life's ambitions. This will be a year that will give you a sense of fulfillment.

This is a lucky year for Sagittarius, but hard work and commitment would be the key to being able to succeed. Don't be shortsighted, learn to look at the big picture. All your moves should be made wisely.

Beginning May 25, Jupiter, your ruler, transits into Gemini. This will help you get closer to your destiny.

During periods of Mercury Retrograde you are likely to want to plan new beginnings and focus on second chances.

During New Moon periods you may be presented with unique opportunities, so you must be very smart with your decisions and have faith in yourself.

During full Moon periods your emotions will be at their peak, you should pay more attention to your desires and needs.

Sagittarius' health will be average for this year. You should be alert and concerned about your general well-being. You will have stages of high stress and anxiety that will greatly affect your health. Unhealthy habits could interfere with your heart health.

Be wary of addictions. Get enough rest and rely more on home-cooked meals than fast food.

The year is favorable for your family life, you will have prosperity and happiness in your home. However, the health of your children may cause you to worry.

Those who wish to have a baby will be able to conceive during the last months of 2024.

Love will blossom, but you must try to resolve any differences that exist in your relationship.

Love

This year you will pay extra attention to your love relationships, as any existing problems may worsen. You must work to remove blockages in love.

During Eclipse periods you can reconnect with old loves. Eclipses can remind you to be cheerful, have fun and let love into your life if you are single.

Full Moon periods will bring you closer to those with whom you have strong ties and with whom you feel a spiritual connection, but you will stay away from toxic people.

Jupiter after May 25 and for the rest of 2024 will bring energy to your relationships. You will have the opportunity to meet many important people and from these new connections a love may arise.

If you are in a relationship, you may decide to commit.

During new Moon periods you will be open to commitment, and to emotional and physical bonds with others. Sentimentality, sensuality, passion, and lots of fun await you.

Economy

Uranus continues to bring changes to your work life, but Jupiter gives you opportunities to make the changes you desire.

You will have new opportunities for projects, or a completely new job that will excite you.

Keep an eye on new Moon periods because it is during them that new opportunities will appear for you to prosper.

You will be more productive, efficient, and organized, and any projects you are involved in will bear a lot of fruit, meaning a lot of money, after August.

During Full Moon periods you will feel emotionally connected to your work or profession. During these periods you will approach the end of important stages for you financially.

You must have financial plans and invest wisely. Don't get carried away with ordinary investment options because you can lose your capital. Jupiter and Saturn favor your long-term investment plans. In general, this is a year in which you will not feel any financial crisis.

Sagittarius Health

As you are such an active sign, you run the risk of not realizing how chronic fatigue and stress accumulate. It is advisable that you dedicate time to relaxation. Massages, chatting with friends, and walking along the beach will improve your mood and your appetite.

A healthy diet is recommended, try to consume enough foods rich in vitamins. Due to deficiency of certain vitamins, you may experience skin problems.

You should avoid nervous tensions and not take on so many responsibilities at once. A vacation by the sea would not only be exciting but will have a good effect on your physical and mental well-being.

Some Sagittarians will have several dental appointments, and others will sadly say goodbye to their favorite foods. You must go on a diet.

Any effort will not be in vain. Moderation and a focus on your health will become sources of optimism.

Family

There may be some nebulous issues in your home, but these events will strengthen your emotional intuition.

Some old problems related to your home and family will have to be eliminated. This may mean several periods of uncertainty, instability, or lack of family connection.

You may move to another location, or buy property, expand the family, or take on large family responsibilities. New Moon periods are the ones that can bring these opportunities.

Be very careful during Lunar Eclipses as this strong energy can amplify any family problems. The smart thing to do would be to try to make things better before the Eclipse.

Important Dates

01/ 02- Mercury transits direct in Sagittarius.

You will be able to communicate more fluently, your thoughts will focus more easily on the future.

05/23- Full Moon in Sagittarius.

You will have the opportunity to let go of ways of thinking that limit your growth. It is the perfect time to broaden your perspective and feel more confident. This Full Moon marks the end of emotional attachments that are out of sync with your energy. A chapter in your life related to financial matters closes. You must find balance in your daily routines.

10/17- Venus transits Sagittarius.

It is the time to conquer as your aura will be magnetic. Seriousness will not be part of your romantic plans and you will have the opportunity to try new things.

11/ 02- Mercury transits Sagittarius.

You will have a clearer understanding of people's motivations and actions.

11/21- Sun enters Sagittarius.

11/ 26- Mercury Retrograde in Sagittarius.

Avoid signing agreements. Reflect on your past, learn to ask for forgiveness and be flexible with your schedule. Plan everything in advance. Don't make important decisions.

12/ 01- New Moon in Sagittarius.

Analyze your personal relationships, take things calmly and free yourself from stress. Eliminate routine, plan new things with effort and dedication. Set solid goals.

12/ 06- Sun conjunct Mercury in Sagittarius.

Perfect day for you to communicate your ideas with clarity and confidence.

12/15- Mercury direct in Sagittarius.

You will be able to communicate more fluently, your thoughts will focus more easily on the future.

Monthly Horoscopes for Sagittarius 2024

January 2024

This month you will receive some extra money, don't waste it. It is always healthy to have an emergency plan in case things go wrong.

It is a month where you should be more present in the lives of the people you love, not that you spend every day with them, but if you take the time to share some days within the month.

In the middle of the month, you will feel very enthusiastic, you should channel that enthusiasm by decorating your home.

You will not be able to reach an agreement with someone at work and unfortunately this situation will drag on for several weeks.

Remember that communication is a very important part of this discussion.

You may wonder if you should say yes to a request made by a person you had not noticed. You should do it because this person will play a special role in your life, and it will mean a singular and necessary story. One of true love.

You are giving up money by not giving up your arm in an unimportant dispute.

Lucky numbers

12-19 -21 -33-36

February 2024

Organize your schedule better so that the necessary sleep time is not affected. Your dreams will only come to guide you if you give them the necessary time and space.

Gifts are an essential part of romance, but those gifts are no substitute for presence and care, quality time and love itself.

If you are alone, don't let it be envy that brings you closer to that person, it was the partner of someone who has unresolved issues with you, but love cannot be revenge.

You will be offered a very good deal by someone who is confident that you will be able to complete it, show your appreciation for being considered for this proposal and try.

Don't forget that you must keep abreast of all the new technologies and new studies that have come out in the profession you are in.

Do not be afraid to love again, the person who has come into your life is making you see things in a different way, but you are afraid to give yourself because of bad experiences you lived, trust more in life.

Lucky numbers

4 - 17 - 20 - 33 - 35

March 2024

This month you will have to make an important decision in love, since probably a person you like very much does not feel the same for you. You should pay attention because there is someone else in your life who has all his attention on you and you have not wanted to give him entrance to your heart, you should analyze well what you want.

You should not fall into erratic behavior just because some of your friends do it, it is not fair to the people who love you. If you are in a moment of weakness of character and want to try things you shouldn't, you should first think about the consequences it will have for your family and for your future.

A mistake you made in the past will come back to haunt you, so you may have to apologize or pay something you owe.

At the end of the month the speed of your thinking accelerates, you will realize that what used to take you hours to process will be done in a few minutes. With this mental predisposition you can achieve many things.

Lucky numbers

2 - 10 - 18 - 19 - 23

April 2024

This month you should not be postponing everything you want to do because of what you have an obligation to do. The time has come to take charge of your life and begin to organize your priorities, which should always include the time to do the things you enjoy.

You can't keep an eye on everyone's life. You must let those around you know that they must make decisions for themselves, as you are not always going to be there to help them.

Someone has been taking advantage of your kindness, you have thought about it, but you have not wanted to accept the truth, it is time to do it, because you can no longer accept that deal where you are not receiving anything in return for your efforts.

Your mind is in a period of immense creativity. You possess a constant thirst for information. Quench your thirst by taking an advanced training course that will help you become better at your profession.

There are people who want to damage your partner's reputation by spreading rumors. You should listen carefully and protect yourself from such people.

Lucky numbers
2 - 8 - 26 - 30 - 33

May 2024

This is a perfect month to negotiate and close deals. Money will come to you in mysterious ways.

Remember that excess is an enemy. Organization will be key this month along with patience and the ability to turn negatives into positives.

You must strive to create balance between home, family, friends, and your financial future.

In the name of love, you must restrain your flirting. Align your heart and desires.

Always try to be on time for work, complete all your tasks and be very responsible.

If you are single, you will have the perfect opportunity to find a new love. If you have a stable relationship, it's time to strengthen those sentimental ties, and if the relationship is long distance, don't forget to show how much you care about your partner.

There may be some discomfort due to liver problems, keep control, limit alcohol, and follow a good diet to relieve your body.

Lucky numbers

5 - 12 - 16 - 22 - 27

June 2024

You are wasting your time and talent; you should not give up because your efforts will be rewarded. Plan your economy if you do not want to have unpleasant surprises. You must take all decisions with great courage.

You've been going through a lot of stress lately and the consequences are starting to emerge. You've had to put up with a lot, but the problems are starting to resolve themselves and it's time for you to take it easy.

Do not underestimate some changes, some of them are positive, but others may not be as favorable as they seem at first glance. Do not rush and analyze the alternatives and prospects of each option.

You are likely to argue with a friend and end up withdrawing your confidence in him. This whole situation is due to nervousness about economic circumstances that should not be allowed to influence you negatively.

Try to internalize opportunities as you are in for a surprise. Walk at your own pace, something big is coming.

Lucky numbers

14 - 17 - 24 - 29 – 30

July 2024

This month remember that your heart and your head should not be in conflict. You may change your place of work this month, do not despair.

You will have the courage to face the problem of an outstanding debt, as well as the ability to negotiate the type of payment plan you can afford.

After the 14th there will be an argument with your partner, he/she will say hurtful things to you. It is up to you to decide whether to continue next to someone capable of hurting you.

In your workplace there are people who do not have your skills and knowledge, but who occupy more important and better paid positions than yours. You feel that your preparation and knowledge are not recognized, and you feel undervalued. All this happens because you do not know how to demand what is rightfully yours. You must fight for what you want and avoid giving in easily.

You should focus on taking a direction on what you want or don't want to do in the future, don't be afraid.

Lucky numbers

6 - 8 - 22 - 25 - 35

August 2024

You don't have the patience required to cultivate long-term relationships. You always want immediate results, that can get in the way of your growth.

You will attend a group party where you and that special someone will leave early to spend some time for an intimate conversation.

To understand the ways of love you must ask your friends for advice. If you want to have a partner, you must take care of it.

A perfect month for those who want to buy a house, at least you must start saving to be able to do so.

There is a person who has a lot of interest in you but is losing it seeing the coldness you behave.

You need to control your expenses; you will probably go over your budget and that will affect you in a way you don't expect.

Lucky numbers

5 - 12 - 21 - 22 - 23

September 2024

This month does not indicate that there will be major changes in your love life. Those in a stable relationship will not experience major changes, and singles are not likely to find their soul mate either.

Whoever you work for may be undergoing major changes and you may even be offered the chance to work abroad or to go on work-related trips.

You will be prone to pay less attention to your health, it is important that you try not to fall into this tendency. A good diet, exercise and a healthy lifestyle will fill you with vitality. You should avoid excesses; you could end up stressed or anxious.

Possibilities for romances outside of your marriage may arise, but this does not mean that you will take advantage of them.

Anyway, your relationship as a couple is being tested, it is important that, when faced with small misunderstandings, you do not withdraw thinking that everything is solved by itself, try to be proactive to solve it by talking and listening.

Lucky numbers
4 - 8 - 12 - 13 - 22

October 2024

This month your work and profession will continue with its inertia. You will think about taking a vacation, for that reason you will not have to work a lot and you will not have to make important decisions.

You will do well financially anyway, but things will evolve slowly. It is not the month for big investments, you should buy the basics for your life without excessive expenses.

You will enjoy exercising and going out at night with your friends.

In love you will do well. If you have a partner, the relationship will progress smoothly. If you are single, it could be a month in which you will be very successful with the opposite sex, so you could have several sporadic relationships. The issue is that you are not clear whether you want to commit or not. Even if you meet someone special, you will let him or her slip away. Your desire to advance and your ambition will make you focused on work at the end of the month, because you want to succeed. Your home will be very quiet, but the challenge of the month is to combine your work with your family.

Lucky numbers

4 - 8 - 12 - 13 - 22

November 2024

This month fatigue and stress will weaken you; you must stay as strong as possible. Sleep well, rest, take vitamins, do whatever is necessary so that it does not affect you too much.

If you are in a relationship, you will feel good, but you will begin to question whether that relationship is really what you need. This will cause you to be focused on your thoughts. If you are alone, it is not a month to start a stable relationship. Not because you won't find interesting people, but because you don't know well what you want.

Economically it is a good period and money will come in easily. Good period to invest in the long term, you should think about your future.

You should take advantage and start planning a vacation, to rest and recharge your batteries. You will need to be in shape for the coming year 2025.

Take care of yourself, it's no use killing yourself doing exercises only to get injured and must be inactive for a while.

Lucky numbers

11 - 12 - 13 - 17 - 25

December 2024

If you have a partner, you will have a good calm, but you will feel that your partner is a little out of sync. This means that you are not in sync, but you should not worry, because it is not your fault, it is she who does not know what she wants. If you are single, it is a good month to meet people. Don't rush into things, take your time to get to know this person well and don't make a mistake.

Money will come to you from various sources, which will fill your bank account to overflowing. If you have investments, they will give you profits. You will feel lucky, and you will be able to treat yourself to some luxuries and whims. People will see you as a millionaire. It is a fantastic month for your economy.

Your home will be very good, as you will do so well with money, you will be able to give them gifts. You will feel loved, and you will notice their unconditional support.

You will have energy to do whatever you want. You will have fun with yourself. Your image will be attractive, and you will feel satisfied. Avoid accidents.

Lucky numbers

2 - 7 - 17 - 25 - 36

The Tarot Cards, an Enigmatic and Psychological World.

The word Tarot means "royal road", it is a millenary practice, it is not known exactly who invented card games in general, nor the Tarot in particular; there are the most dissimilar hypotheses in this sense.

Some say that it arose in Atlantis or Egypt, but others believe that tarots came from China or India, from the ancient land of the gypsies, or that they arrived in Europe through the Cathars. The fact is that tarot cards distill astrological, alchemical, esoteric, and religious symbolism, both Christian and pagan.

Until recently, if you mentioned the word 'tarot' to some people, it was common for them to imagine a gypsy sitting in front of a crystal ball in a room surrounded by mysticism, or to think of black magic or witchcraft, but nowadays this has changed.

This ancient technique has been adapting to the new times, it has joined technology and many young people feel a deep interest in it.

Young people have isolated themselves from religion because they believe that they will not find the solution to what they need there, they realized the duality of this, something that does not happen with spirituality. All over the social networks you find accounts dedicated to the study and tarot readings, since everything related to esotericism is fashionable, in fact, some hierarchical decisions are made considering the tarot or astrology.

What is remarkable is that the predictions that are usually related to tarot are not the most sought after, the ones related to self-knowledge and spiritual counseling are the most requested.

The tarot is an oracle, through its drawings and colors, we stimulate our psychic sphere, the innermost part that goes beyond the natural. Many people turn to the tarot as a spiritual or psychological guide because we live in uncertain times, and this pushes us to seek answers in spirituality.

It is such a powerful tool that tells you concretely what is going on in your subconscious so that you can perceive it through the lens of a new wisdom.

Carl Gustav Jung, the famed psychologist, used the symbols of tarot cards in his psychological studies. He created the theory of archetypes, where he discovered an extensive sum of images that help in analytical psychology.

The use of drawings and symbols to appeal to a deeper understanding is frequently used in psychoanalysis. These allegories are part of us, corresponding to symbols of our subconscious and our mind.

Our unconscious has dark areas, and when we use visual techniques, we can reach different parts of it and reveal elements of our personality that we do not know. When you can decode these messages through the pictorial language of tarot, you can choose what decisions to make in life to create the destiny you really want.

The tarot with its symbols teaches us that a different universe exists, especially nowadays where everything is so chaotic, and a logical explanation is sought for everything.

Wheel of Fortune Tarot Card for Sagittarius 2024

Favorable change, luck, new conditions, and improvements.

Success and evolution thanks to your creativity, luck in games of chance, balance between opposing forces. This card represents the principle of polarity that leads us to face changes with courage.

It symbolizes the cycles of life and speaks of new beginnings, transformations governed by destiny and, therefore, out of your control.

The desire for adventure, spontaneity, and good humor.

It portends victories and success. However, you must remember that nothing comes on a silver platter.

Even if success comes knocking at your door, you must continue to strive for it.

It means a well-deserved victory.

It symbolizes hard work and dedication, indicating that success will not come easy, you must earn it.

You must take charge of your destiny and prepare to take advantage of the opportunities that this year 2024 will give you.

Runes of the Year 2024

Runes are a set of symbols that form an alphabet. "Rune" means secret and symbolizes the noise of one stone colliding with another. Runes are an ancient visionary and magical method.

Runes do not serve for exact predictions, but they do serve to guide you about a future event, a subject, or a decision.

The runes have a specific meaning for the person who wants it, but also some message related to the adversities that arise in life.

Thurisaz, Rune of Sagittarius 2024

This is the year to make decisions. However, remember that a hasty decision causes serious mistakes. Therefore, avoid impulsive acts, try not to do anything that exceeds your capabilities. In other words, think well before you act.

There are always external factors beyond your control, so you must be tolerant.

You still have a long way to go, you should wait and, before taking the first step, analyze the situation, the past, your mistakes and successes. Then when the time comes you will be able to make the right decision.

Do not act until conditions are favorable.

The work you must do is not only external, but you must also calmly review your heart and soul.

Analyze how you have arrived now and visualize the achievements and challenges before acting.

Thurisaz warns you that what you are really facing is the reflection of what is hidden in your subconscious.

The energy of the conflict you are going through is neutral, for that reason you must accept the dynamics involved.

This rune announces that you are protected and that you have the power to face any obstacle.

Lucky Colors

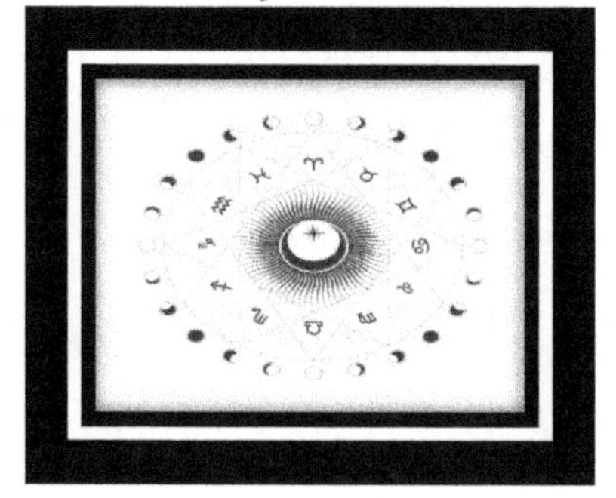

Colors affect us psychologically; they influence our appreciation of things, opinion about something or someone, and can be used to influence our decisions.

Traditions to welcome the new year vary from country to country, and on the night of December 31 we take stock of all the positive and negative things we experienced in the year that is leaving. We start thinking about what to do to transform our luck in the new year ahead.

There are several ways to attract positive energies towards us when we receive the new year, and one of them is to wear or wear accessories of a specific color that attracts what we wish for the year that is about to begin.

Colors have energetic charges that influence our lives, so it is always advisable to receive the year dressed in a color that attracts the energies of what we want to achieve.

For that there are colors that vibrate positively with each zodiac sign, so the recommendation is that you wear the clothes with the hue that will make you attract prosperity, health, and love in 2024. (These colors can also be used during the rest of the year for important occasions, or to enhance your days).

Remember that, although the most common is to wear red underwear for passion, pink for love and yellow or gold for abundance, it is never too much to include in our attire the color that most benefits our zodiac sign.

Sagittarius

Orange

The key words for orange are *energy, joy, happiness, and creativity.*

Orange is a cheerful color that helps to release negative emotions. Using it will make you feel confident, and sympathetic to other people's shortcomings.

Orange is a color that stimulates the mind, renews illusions and is antidepressant.

Orange is widely used in Buddhism, as it is associated with the sacral chakra, and is related to sexuality, creativity, and passion. This chakra is associated with the water element and helps to balance emotions and increase vital energies.

Lucky Charms

Who doesn't own a lucky ring, a chain that never comes off, or an object that they wouldn't give away for anything in the world? We all attribute a special power to certain items that belong to us and that special character that they assume for us makes them magical objects.

For a talisman to act and influence circumstances, its bearer must have faith in it, and this will transform it into a prodigious object, able to accomplish everything that is asked of it.

Usually, an amulet is any object that propitiates good as a preventive measure against evil, harm, disease, and witchcraft.

Amulets for good luck can help you to have a year 2024 full of blessings in your home, work, with your family, attract money and health. For the amulets to work properly you should not lend them to anyone else, and you should always have them at hand.

Amulets have existed in all cultures and are made from elements of nature that serve as catalysts of energies that help create human desires.

The amulet is assigned the power to ward off evils, spells, diseases, disasters or to counteract evil wishes cast through the eyes of others.

Amulet for Sagittarius

Horse

Horses are considered symbols of wealth. In ancient times horses were given as gifts to emperors and kings because they are symbols of triumph and success.

Horses signify power, strength, and courage. They are a symbol of speed, courage, and perseverance.

They are associated with the Fire element and represent fame, freedom and achievement of goals that require your energetic strength.

You can put ornaments with the figure of a horse, or several in the living room, study, office or if you work at home place it on your desk. As it is considered an amulet to attract success and good luck it must be near you.

Lucky Quartz

We are all attracted to diamonds, rubies, emeralds and sapphires, obviously precious stones. Semi-precious stones such as carnelian, tiger's eye, white quartz, and lapis lazuli are also highly prized as they have been used as ornaments and symbols of power for thousands of years.

What many do not know is that they were valued for more than their beauty: each had a sacred significance, and their healing properties were as important as their ornamental value.

Crystals still have the same properties in our days, most people are familiar with the most popular ones such as amethyst, malachite and obsidian, but nowadays there are new crystals such as larimar, petalite and phenacite that have become known.

A crystal is a solid body with a geometrically regular shape, crystals were formed when the earth was created and have continued to metamorphose as the planet has changed, crystals are the DNA of the earth, they are miniature stores that contain the development of our planet over millions of years.

Some have been bent to extraordinary pressures and others grew in chambers buried deep underground, others dripped into being. Whatever form they take, their crystalline structure can absorb, conserve, focus and emit energy.

At the heart of the crystal is the atom, its electrons, and protons. The atom is dynamic and is composed of a series of particles that rotate around the center in constant motion, so that, although the crystal may seem motionless, it is a living molecular mass that vibrates at a certain frequency, and this is what gives energy to the crystal.

Gems used to be a royal and priestly prerogative, the priests of Judaism wore a plaque on their chest full of precious stones which was much more than an emblem to designate their function, as it transferred power to the wearer.

Men have worn stones since the stone age as they had a protective function guarding their wearers from various evils. Today's crystals have the same power, and we can select our jewelry not only according to their external attractiveness, having them near us can boost our energy (orange carnelian), clean the space around us (amber) or attract wealth (citrine).

Certain crystals such as smoky quartz and black tourmaline can absorb negativity, emitting a pure and clean energy.

Wearing a black tourmaline around the neck protects from electromagnetic emanations including that of cell phones, a citrine will not only attract wealth, but will also help you keep it, place it in the wealthy part of your home (the back left most away from the front door).

If you are looking for love, crystals can help you, place a rose quartz in the relationship corner of your house (the back right corner furthest away from the front door) its effect is so powerful that you may want to add an amethyst to offset the attraction.

You can also use rhodochrosite, love will come your way.

Crystals can heal and give balance, some crystals contain minerals known for their therapeutic properties, malachite has a high concentration of copper, wearing a malachite bracelet allows the body to absorb minimal amounts of copper.

Lapis lazuli relieves migraine, but if the headache is caused by stress, amethyst, amber or turquoise placed above the eyebrows will relieve it.

Quartz and minerals are jewels of mother earth, give yourself the opportunity, and connect with the magic they give off.

Lucky Charm for Sagittarius

Agate

A quartz with great energetic power. It helps to increase self-esteem and transforms negative energies into positive ones.

It helps emotional, mental, and physical stability. It is good for migraines, relieves all kinds of physical ailments, such as muscle, joint and bone pain.

It is known as the stone of confidence. It will bring you wealth and abundance in all areas of your life.

It helps to develop creativity and security. It is also assigned powers to evade curses.

If you place it under your pillow, you will not have problems to sleep, you will avoid insomnia, stress at night, or anxieties.

It will give you a calculating mentality.

It acts as an amulet so that things go well, and you obtain prosperity in a short period of time.

To take advantage of the protective qualities of this quartz you should always have it with you.

Rituals 2024

In this book we offer you several spells and rituals so that you can attract economic abundance to your life in the year 2024, because this will be a year of many challenges.

When everything is going downhill, spiritual help is timely.

Magic works. Most successful people, unbelievably, practice it, of course they will not tell you. They have achieved their triumphs because they have carefully performed some of the rituals, we offer you in this book.

If you got tired of failing in love in the last years, you have acquired the right book, because your love life will totally change when you perform the rituals we recommend.

Health spells and white magic rituals will help you to maintain or improve your health, but never forget that they do not replace any doctor, nor the treatments they prescribe.

Health spells are extremely popular in the world of magic, after love or money spells, health spells are in great demand due to their high effectiveness, although they are not easy to cast because health is a delicate subject.

There are infinite reasons why a ritual or spell may not work, and without realizing it, we make mistakes.

Ritual energy is wasted if too many people know what you are doing.

To achieve positive results, we must practice them at the right time.

These magical periods are related to astrology, and we must know them and program our rituals for these periods of time that will be the most appropriate to perform our magic.

Rituals for the Month of January

January 2024

Sunday	Monday	Tuesday	Wednesday	Thursday	Friday	Saturday
	1	**2**	**3**	**4**	**5**	**6**
7	**8**	**9**	**10**	**11** New Moon	**12**	**13**
14	**15**	**16**	**17**	**18**	**19**	**20**
21	**22**	**23**	**24**	**25** Full Moon	**26**	**27**
28	**29**	**30**	**31**			

January 11, 2024, Capricorn New Moon 20°44'.

January 25, 2024, Full Moon   Leo5°14

Best money rituals

Thursday, January 11, 2024 *(Jupiter day). New Moon in Capricorn, a sign of stability. Good day to organize our goals, our vocations, our career, to obtain honors. To ask for a raise, to make presentations, public speaking. For spells related to work or money. Rituals related to getting promotions, relationships with superiors and achieving success.*

Thursday, January 25, 2024 *(Venus's day) Favorable for money spells, love, and legal matters. Rituals related to prosperity and obtaining jobs.*

Ritual for Luck in Games of Chance

On a lottery ticket you write the amount of money you want to win on the front of the ticket and on the back your name. Burn the ticket with a green candle. Collect the ashes in a purple paper and bury them.

Make Money with the Moon Cup. Full Moon

You need:
- 1 crystal glass
- 1 large plate

- Fine sand
- Gold glitter
- 4 cups sea salt
- 1 malachite quartz
- 1 cup of sea, river, or sacred water
- Cinnamon sticks or cinnamon powder
- Dried or fresh basil
- Fresh or dried parsley
- Corn kernels
- 3 bills of current denomination

Place the three folded bills, cinnamon sticks, corn kernels, malachite, basil, and parsley inside the glass. Mix the glitter with the sand and add it to the glass until it is filled. Under the light of the Full Moon, place the plate with the four cups of sea salt.

Place the cup in the middle of the plate, surrounded by the salt. Pour the cup of sacred water on the plate, so that it moistens the salt well, leave it all night in the light of the Full Moon, and part of the day until the water vaporizes and the salt is dry again.

Add four or five grains of salt to the glass and pour the rest.

Take the cup inside your home, somewhere visible or where you keep your money.

Every full moon day you will spread a little of the contents of the cup in every corner of your house and sweep it up the next day.

Best Rituals for Love

Friday, January 19, 2024 *(Venus Day). Appropriate for spells or rituals related to love, contracts, and partnerships.*

Spell to Sweeten Your Loved One

You print the full name of the person you love and yours on top of it seven times on brown paper.

You place this paper inside a crystal glass and put honey, cinnamon, a rose quartz, and pieces of orange peel.

While performing the ritual repeat in your mind: "I sweeten you and only true love reigns between us". Keep it in a dark place.

Ritual to Attract Love

You need.

- Rose oil

- 1 rose quartz

- 1 apple

- 1 red rose in a small vase

- 1 white rose in a small vase

- 1 long red ribbon

- 1 red candle

For maximum effectiveness, this ritual should be performed on a Friday or Sunday at the time of the planet Venus or Jupiter.

You must consecrate the candle before starting the ritual with rose oil. Light the candle. Cut the apple into two pieces and place one in the red rose vase and the other in the white rose vase. Tie the red ribbon around the two vases. Leave them all night next to the candle until the candle burns out. While you perform this operation repeat in your mind: "May the person who is destined to make me happy appear in my path, I receive and accept it".

When the roses dry, together with the apple halves bury them in your yard or in a pot with the rose quartz.

To Attract an Impossible Love

You need:
- 1 red rose
- 1 white rose
- 1 red candle
- 1 white candle
- 3 yellow candles
- Glass fountain
- Pentacle # 4 of Venus

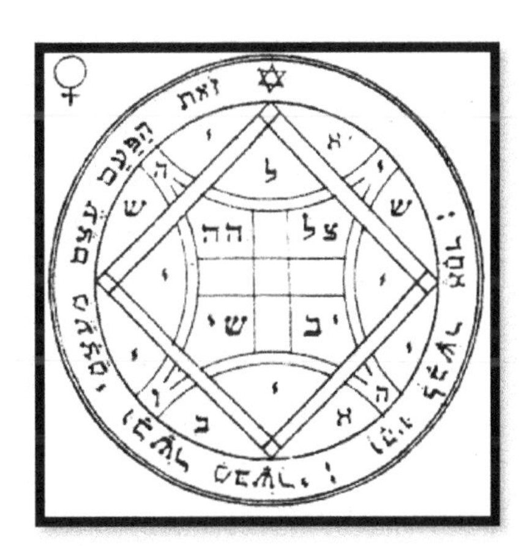

Pentacle #4 of Venus.

You must place the yellow candles in the shape of a triangle. Write on the back of the Venus pentacle your wishes about love and the name of the person you want in your life, place the fountain on top of the pentacle in the middle. Light the red and white candle and put them in the fountain together with the roses. You repeat this phrase: "Universe divert towards my heart the light of (full name)'s love".

You repeat this three times. When the candles are extinguished, you take everything to the courtyard and bury it.

Best Rituals for Health

Tuesday, January 30, 2024 (Mars Day). *To protect yourself or recover your health.*

Spell to Protect the Health of our Pets.

Boil mineral water, thyme, rosemary, and mint. When it cools, place it in a spray bottle in front of a green and a golden candle.

When the candles are consumed you should use this spray on your pet for nine days. On the chest and back.

Immediate Improvement Spell

You must get a white candle, a green candle, and a yellow candle.

You will consecrate them (from the base to the wick) with pine essence and place them on a table with a light blue tablecloth, in the shape of a triangle.

In the center, you will place a small glass container with alcohol and a small amethyst.

At the base of the container a piece of paper with the name of the sick person or photo with his/her full name on the back and date of birth.

You light the three candles and leave them burning until they are completely consumed.

While performing this ritual visualize the person completely healthy.

Slimming Spell

You must prick your finger with a pin and put 3 drops of your blood and a spoonful of sugar on a white paper, then close the paper wrapping the blood with the sugar.

You place this paper in a new glass container, fill the glass halfway with your urine, leave it overnight in front of a white candle and bury it the next day.

Rituals for the Month of February

February 2024

Sunday	Monday	Tuesday	Wednesday	Thursday	Friday	Saturday
				1	**2**	**3**
4	**5**	**6**	**7**	**8**	**9** New Moon	**10**
11	**12**	**13**	**14**	**15**	**16**	**17**
18	**19**	**20**	**21**	**22**	**23** Full Moon	**24**
25	**26**	**27**	**28**	**29**		

February 9, 2024, Aquarius New Moon 20°40'.

February 23, 2024, Full Moon Virgo 5°22'.

Best money rituals

February 9, 2024 (Venus Day). In this phase we work to increase or attract anything. In this cycle we make requests for love to come, to increase the money in our accounts or our work prestige.

Ritual to Increase Clientele. Gibbous Crescent Moon

You need:

- *5 rue leaves*
- *5 verbena leaves*
- *5 rosemary leaves*
- *5 grains of coarse sea salt*
- *5 coffee beans*
- *5 grains of wheat*
- *1 magnet stone*
- *1 white cloth bag*
- *Red thread*
- *Red ink*
- *1 business card*
- *1 pot with a large green plant*
- *4 citrine quartz*

Place all the materials inside the white bag, except for the magnet, the card, and the citrines. Next, sew it with red thread, then print the name of the business on the outside with red ink. Leave the bag under the counter or in a drawer in your desk for a full week.

After this time, you bury it at the bottom of the pot with the magnet stone and the business card. Finally, place the four citrines on top of the earth of the pot in the direction of the four cardinal points.

Prosperity Spell

You need:

- 3 pyrites or citrine quartz

- 3 gold coins

- 1 gold candle

- 1 red sachet

On the first day of the New Moon, you place a table near a window; on the table you will place the coins and the quartz in the form of a triangle. You light the candle, place it in the middle and looking at the sky you repeat three times the following prayer:

"Moon that illuminates my life, use the power you have to attract money to me and make these coins multiply."

When the candle is consumed, put the coins and quartz with the right hand in the red bag, carry it always with you, it will be your talisman to attract money, no one should touch it.

Best Rituals for Love

February 11, 22, 25, 2024. For spells or rituals related to love, contracts, and partnerships.

Ritual to Consolidate Love

This spell is most effective during the Full Moon phase.

You need:

- 1 wooden box
- Photographs
- Honey
- Red rose petals
- 1 amethyst quartz
- Cinnamon stick

You should take the photographs, print their full names and dates of birth, place them inside the box so that they are facing each other.

Add the honey, rose petals, amethyst, and cinnamon.

Place the box under your bed for thirteen days. After this time remove the amethyst from the box and wash it with Moon water.

You should keep it with you as an amulet to attract the love you long for. The rest you should take it to a river or a forest.

Ritual to Rescue a Love in Decay

You need:
- 2 red candles
- 1 piece of yellow paper
- 1 red envelope
- 1 red pencil
- 1 photo of the loved one and a photo of you
- 1 metal container
- 1 red ribbon
- New sewing needle

This ritual is most effective during the Crescent Moon phase and on a Friday at the time of the planet Venus or the Sun. You should consecrate your candles with rose oil or cinnamon.

You write on the yellow paper with the red pencil your name and your partner's name. You also write what you wish with short but precise words. Print the names on each candle with the sewing needle. Light the candles and place the paper between the photos face to face and tie them with the ribbon. Burn the photos in the metal container with the candle that has your name on it and repeat aloud:

"Our is strengthened by the force of the universe and all the energies that exist throughout time".

Place the ashes in the envelope and when the candles are consumed, place the envelope under your mattress at the headboard.

Best Rituals for Health

February 4,12,19, 2024. Advisable periods for surgical interventions since it favors the healing capacity.

Ritual for Health

Boil several white rose petals, rosemary, and rue in a pot. When it cools, add rose essence and almond oil. Light five purple candles in your bathroom, which you have previously consecrated with orange and eucalyptus oil. On one candle you should print the name of the person. Take a bath with this water and while you are bathing, you must visualize that diseases will not come near you or your family.

Ritual for the Health in the Crescent Moon Phase

In an aluminum foil you will place sea salt, 3 cloves of garlic, four bay leaves, five leaves of rue, a black tourmaline, and a piece of paper with the name of the person. Fold it and tie it with a purple ribbon. Carry this amulet with you in your jacket pocket or purse.

Rituals for the Month of March

March 2024

Sunday	Monday	Tuesday	Wednesday	Thursday	Friday	Saturday
					1	**2**
3	**4**	**5**	**6**	**7**	**8**	**9**
10 New Moon	**11**	**12**	**13**	**14**	**15**	**16**
17	**18**	**19**	**20**	**21**	**22**	**23**
24 Full Moon	**25**	**26**	**27**	**28**	**29**	**30**
31						

March 10, 2024, Pisces New Moon 20°16'.

March 24, 2024, Full Moon Libra 5°07' (Penumbral Lunar Eclipse 5°13')

Best money rituals

March 8,10,22, 2024. Rituals related to prosperity and obtaining jobs.

Spell for Success in Job Interviews.

Place in a green bag three leaves of sage, basil, parsley, and rue. Add a tiger eye quartz and a malachite.

Close the bag with a golden ribbon. To activate it you put it in your left hand at the level of your heart and then a few centimeters above you put your right hand, close your eyes, and imagine a white energy coming out of your right hand towards your left hand covering the bag.

You keep it in your wallet or pocket.

Ritual so that Money is always Present in your Home.

You need a white glass bottle, black beans, red beans, sunflower seeds, corn kernels, wheat kernels and a myrrh incense.

You put everything in the bottle in the same order, close it with a cork lid and pour the smoke from the incense. Then you place it as a decoration in your kitchen.

Gypsy Spell for Prosperity

Get a medium-sized clay pot and paint it green. In the bottom put some myrrh, a coin, and a few drops of olive oil. Cover it with a layer of soil and place seeds of your favorite plant. Add cinnamon and more soil. You should keep it in the dining room of your house and water it so that it grows.

Best rituals for love

March 1, 17, 24, 29, 2024

Ritual to Away Relationship Problems

This ritual should be practiced during the Lunar Eclipse or the Full Moon phase.

You need:
- 1 white ribbon

- 1 new scissors
- 1 red ink ballpoint pen

You should write on the white ribbon with the red ink the problem you are having and the name of the person. Then you cut it into seven pieces with the scissors and while doing so you repeat aloud:

"This is my problem. I want you to leave and never come back. Please take it away from me. That's right."

Place everything inside a black bag and bury it.

Love Bindings

You need:

- Good grass

- Basil

- Full body photo of your loved one without glasses

- Full body photo of you without glasses

- 1 yellow silk handkerchief

- 1 wooden box

Place inside the box the two photographs with the name written on the back of each one.

Put the yellow handkerchief inside and sprinkle the basil and the good herb. Leave it exposed to the energies of the Moon.

The next day bury it in a place that no one knows, when you are opening the hole visualize what you want. When the Full Moon arrives, dig up the box and throw it in a river or in the sea.

Best Rituals for Health

Any day but Saturday.

Spell against Depression

You should take a fig with your right hand and place it in the left side of your mouth without chewing or swallowing it.

Then you take a grape with your left hand and place it in the right side of your mouth without chewing it. When you have both fruits in your mouth you bite them at the same time and swallow them, the fructose they emanate will give you energy and joy.

Recovery Spell

Necessary Elements:

-1 white or pink candle

-Rose petals

-Eucalyptus oil

-Lemon oil

-Orange Oil

You must write with a sewing needle the name of the person who needs the spell. Consecrate the candle with the oils under the full moon, while repeating: "Earth, Air, Fire, Water bring Peace, Health, Joy, and Love to the life of (you say the name of the person)". Let the candle burn out completely. The remains can be discarded anywhere.

Rituals for the Month of April

April 2024

Sunday	Monday	Tuesday	Wednesday	Thursday	Friday	Saturday
	1	**2**	**3**	**4**	**5**	**6**
7	**8** New Moon	**9**	**10**	**11**	**12**	**13**
14	**15**	**16**	**17**	**18**	**19**	**20**
21	**22** Full Moon	**23**	**24**	**25**	**26**	**27**
28	**29**	**30**				

April 8, 2024, New Moon, and Total Solar Eclipse in Aries19°22 '.

April 22, 2024, Full Scorpio Moon 23°:48'.

April 8, 7, 13, 22, 2024

Spell Open Pathways to Abundance.

You need:
- Laurel
- Romero
- 3 gold coins
- 1 gold candle
- silver candle
- 1 white candle

Perform after 24 hours of the New Moon.

Place the candles in the shape of a pyramid, place a coin next to each one and the laurel and rosemary leaves in the middle of this triangle. Light the candles in this order: first the silver, white and gold. Repeat this invocation: "By the power of purifying energy and infinite energy I invoke the help of all the entities that protect me to heal my economy".

Let the candles burn out completely and keep the coins in your wallet; these three coins cannot be spent. When the laurel and rosemary are dry, burn them and pass the smoke of this incense through your home or business.

Best Rituals for Love

April 2, 13, 17, 2024

Moroccan Love Ties

You need:
- Saliva of the other person
- Other person's blood
- Earth
- Rose water
- 1 red handkerchief
- Red thread
- 1 rose quartz
- 1 black tourmaline

Place the red handkerchief on a table. Place the earth on top of the handkerchief and on top place the saliva, the rose quartz, the black tourmaline, and the blood of the person you want to attract.

Sprinkle rose water on everything and tie the handkerchief with the red thread, taking care that the components do not come off. You must bury this handkerchief.

Spell to Sweeten Your Loved One

You print the full name of the person you love and yours on top of it seven times on a brown paper. Place this paper inside a crystal glass and add honey, cinnamon, a rose quartz, and pieces of orange peel. While you perform the ritual repeat in your mind: "I sweeten you and only true love reigns between us". Keep it in a dark place.

Rituals for the Month of May

May 2024

Sunday	Monday	Tuesday	Wednesday	Thursday	Friday	Saturday
			1	**2**	**3**	**4**
5	**6**	**7**	**8** New Moon	**9**	**10**	**11**
12	**13**	**14**	**15**	**16**	**17**	**18**
19	**20**	**21**	**22** Full Moon	**23**	**24**	**25**
26	**27**	**28**	**29**	**30**	**31**	

May 8, 2024, Taurus New Moon 18°01'.

May 22, 2024, Full Moon Sagittarius 2°54'.

Best money rituals

May 6, 13, 21, 25, 2024

"Money Magnet" Crescent Moon

You need:

- 1 empty wine glass

- 2 green candles

- 1 handful of white rice

- 12 legal tender coins

- 1 magnet

- White rice

You light the two candles that should be located one on each side of the wine glass. At the bottom of the glass, you put the magnet. Then you take a handful of white rice and place it in the glass. Then place the twelve coins inside the glass.

When the candles are consumed to the end, place the coins in the prosperity corner of your home or business.

Spell to Cleanse Negativity in your Home or Business.

You need:

- *Egg shell*
- *1 bouquet of white flowers*
- *Sacred water or Full Moon water*
- *Milk*
- *Cinnamon Powder*
- *New cleaning bucket*
- *New mop*

You start by sweeping your home or business from the inside to the outside of the street repeating in your mind to let the negative out and the positive in. You mix all the ingredients in the bucket and wipe the floor from the inside to the outside of the street door.

You let the floor dry and sweep the flowers towards the street door, pick them up and throw them in the trash along with the bucket and mop.

Do not touch anything with your hands. You should do this once a week, preferably at the time of the planet Jupiter.

Best Rituals for Love

May 22 Full Moon.

Unbreakable Bond of Love

You need:
- 1 Green ribbon
- 1 red marker

You should take the green ribbon and print your full name and the name of the person you love in red ink. Then you write the words: love, Venus, and passion three times. You tie the ribbon to the head of your bed and every night you tie a knot for nine consecutive nights. After this time, you tie the ribbon with three knots on your left arm. When it breaks you burn it and throw the ashes in the sea or in a place where the water runs.

Ritual so that I only Love You

This ritual is most effective if you perform it during the phase of the waxing Gibbous Moon and on a Friday at the time of the planet Venus.

You need:
- 1 tablespoon of honey
- 1 Pentacle # 5 of Venus.
- 1 ballpoint pen with red ink
- 1 white candle
- 1 new sewing needle

Pentacle #5 of Venus.

You must write on the back of the Venus pentacle with the red ink the full name of the person you love and how you want her to behave with you, you must be specific. Then wet it with the honey and roll it around the candle so that it sticks to the candle. Secure it with the sewing needle. When the candle is consumed you bury the remains and repeat aloud: "The love of (name) belongs only to me".

Tea to Forget a Love

You need:
- 5 mint leaves
- 1 tablespoon of honey
- 3 cinnamon sticks

In a cup of water, you should boil all the ingredients, let it rest. Drink it thinking about all the damage this person did to you. Men should take it on Tuesday or Wednesday night before going to bed and women on Monday or Friday before going to bed.

Nail Ritual for Love

You must cut your fingernails and toenails and place them in a metal pot over medium heat to toast all the residues of these nails. You take it out and grind them into powder. This powder you will give it to your partner in your drink or meal.

.

Best Rituals for Health

Any day in May 2024. Except Saturdays.

Magic Formula for Glowing Skin

Mix eight tablespoons of honey, eight teaspoons of olive oil, eight tablespoons of brown sugar, a grated lemon peel and four drops of lemon. When it becomes a smooth mass, apply it all over your body and massage for five minutes.

Then you bathe and alternate between hot and chilly water.

Spell for Cure Toothache

You must make with sea salt a five-pointed star, big because you must stand in the center of it.

On each tip you place a black candle and the symbol of the tetragrammaton (you can print the image), rosemary leaves, bay leaves, apple peels and lavender leaves.

When it is 12:00am you stand in the center, light the candles and repeat:

sanus ossa mea sunt: et labia circa dentes meos

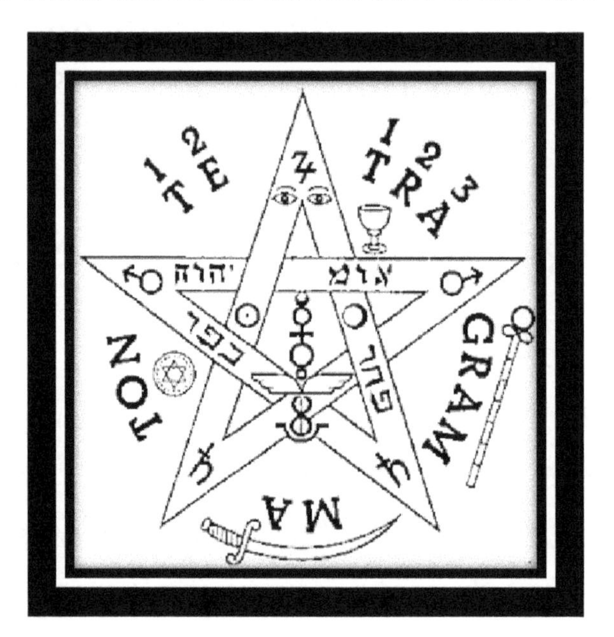

Symbol of the Tetragrammaton

Rituals for the Month of June

June 2024

Sunday	Monday	Tuesday	Wednesday	Thursday	Friday	Saturday
						1
2	3	4	5	6 New Moon	7	8
9	10	11	12	13	14	15
16	17	18	19	20 Full Moon	21	22
23	24	25	26	27	28	29
30						

June 6, 2024, Gemini New Moon 16°17'.

June 20, 2024, Full Moon Capricorn 1°06'.

Best money rituals

6,13,20, 27 are Thursdays, Jupiter days.

Gypsy Prosperity Spell

.

Get a medium-sized clay pot and paint it green. In the bottom put some myrrh, a coin, and a few drops of olive oil. Cover it with a layer of soil and place seeds of your favorite plant. Add cinnamon and more soil. You should keep it in the dining room of your house and water it so that it grows.

Magic Fumigation to improve your Home Economy.

You must light three coals in a metal or clay container and add a spoonful of cinnamon, rosemary, and dried apple peels. You pass it around the house walking clockwise.

Then place white rose petals in a bucket of water and let it stand for three hours.

With this water you will clean your home.

Miracle Essence to Attract Work.

In a dark glass bottle place 32 drops of alcohol, 20 drops of rose water, 10 drops of lavender water and some jasmine leaves.

You shake it several times thinking about what you want to attract.

You put it in a diffuser, you can use it for your home, business or as a personal perfume.

Spell to Wash our Hands and Attract Money.

You need a clay pot, honey, and Full Moon water.

Wash your hands with this liquid but keep the water inside the pan.

Then leave the pot in front of a prosperous business or gambling casino.

Best Rituals *for* Love

Any day in June 2024. Except Saturdays.

Ritual to Prevent Separations

You need:
- 1 pot with red flowers
- Honey
- Pentacle # 1 of Venus
- 1 red pyramid candle
- Photograph of the loved one
- 7 yellow candles

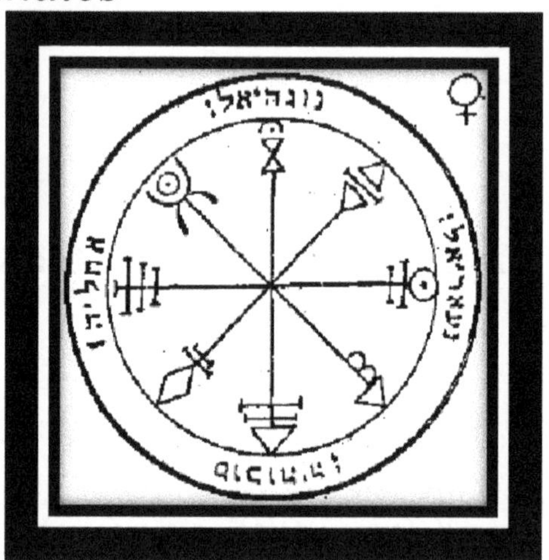

Pentacle #1 of Venus.

You must light the seven yellow candles in the form of a circle. Then you write behind the pentacle of Venus the following incantation:

"I beg you to love me all this life, my dearest love" and the name of the other person. You bury this pentacle in the flowerpot after folding it in five parts

together with the photo. Light the red candle and pour the honey on the soil of the pot.

While performing this operation you repeat aloud the following incantation: "Thanks to the power of Love, we pray, for that (person's name), with a sense of true love that is mine, be preserved so that no one and no force can separate us".

When the candles burn out you throw the remains in the trash. You keep the pot within your reach and take care of it.

Erotic Spell

You must get a red candle in the shape of a penis or vagina (depending on the sex of the person casting the spell). You print the name of the other person on it.

You must consecrate it with sunflower oil and cinnamon.

You should light it once a day, letting it burn only two centimeters.

When the candle is completely consumed, place the remains inside a red cloth bag together with the pentacle #4 of Mars.

This sachet should be kept under your mattress for fifteen days.

After this time, you can throw it away in the garbage.

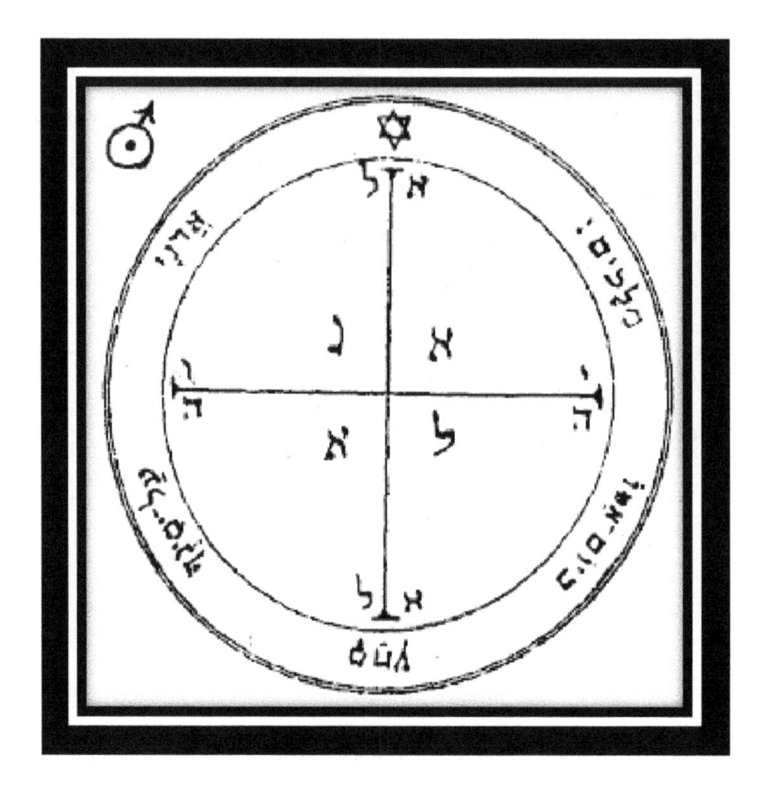

Pentacle #4 Mars

Ritual with Eggs for Attraction

You need:
- 4 eggs
- Yellow paint

You must paint the four eggs yellow and write this word "he comes to me".

You take two eggs and break them in the front corners of the house of the person you want to attract.

You break another egg in front of this person's house. On the third day you throw the fourth egg in a river.

African Spell for Love

You need:
- 1 egg
- 5 red candles
- 1 black handkerchief
- Pumpkin
- Cinnamon oil
- 5 sewing needles
- Bee honey
- Olive Oil
- 5 pieces of bread dough
- Guinea pepper

You open a hole in the pumpkin, after you have printed the full name of the person you want to attract on a piece of paper cartridge, you insert it inside the pumpkin.

Pierce the pumpkin with the needles repeating the name of this person. Pour the rest of the ingredients inside the pumpkin and wrap it in the black scarf. Leave the pumpkin wrapped in this way for five days in front of the red candles, one per day. On the sixth day you bury the pumpkin on the bank of a river.

Best Rituals for Health

Any day in June 2024

Slimming Spell

You must prick your finger with a pin and put 3 drops of your blood and a spoonful of sugar on a white paper, then close the paper wrapping the blood with the sugar.

You place this paper in a new, glass container, fill the glass halfway with your urine, leave it overnight in front of a white candle and bury it the next day.

Spell to Maintain Good Health

Necessary elements.

-1 white candle.

-1 holy card of the Angel of your devotion.

-3 sandalwood incense.

-Vegetable carbons.

-Dried herbs of eucalyptus and basil.

-A handful of rice, a handful of wheat.

-1 white plate or tray.

-8 pink rose petals.

-1 perfume bottle, personal.

-1 wooden box.

You should clean the environment by lighting the vegetable coals in a metal container. When the coals are well lit, you will place little by little the dry herbs on them and go around the room with the container, so that the negative energies are eliminated.

Once the incense is finished, you must open the windows so that the smoke dissipates.

Prepare an altar on a table covered with a white tablecloth. Place the chosen holy card on it and around it places the three incenses in the shape of a triangle. You must consecrate the white candle, then light it and place it in front of the angel together with the uncovered perfume.

You must be relaxed, for that you must concentrate on your breathing. Visualize your angel and thank her for all the good health you have and will always have, this gratitude must come from deep in your heart.

After having made the thanksgiving, you will give him as an offering the handful of rice and the handful of wheat, which you should place inside the tray or white plate.

Scatter over the altar all the rose petals, giving thanks again for the favors received. Once the thanksgiving is finished, leave the candle burning until it is completely consumed. The last thing to do is to gather all the remains of the candle, the incense, the rice, and the wheat, and place them in a plastic bag and throw it in a place where there are trees without the bag.

Place the angel stamp together with the rose petals inside the box and place it in a safe place in your home. The energized perfume, use it when you feel the energies are going down, while visualizing your angel and asking for her protection.

Protective Bath before a Surgical Operation

Necessary elements:

- Purple Bell

- Coconut Water

- Husk

- Cologne 1800

- Always Alive

- Mint Leaves

- Rue leaves

- Rosemary Leaves

- White Candle

- Lavender Oil

Boil all the plants in the coconut water, when it cools, strain it, and add the husk, cologne, lavender oil and light the candle in the west part of your bathroom. Pour the mixture into the bath water. If you do not have a bathtub, pour it over yourself and do not dry yourself.

Rituals for the Month of July

July 2024

Sunday	Monday	Tuesday	Wednesday	Thursday	Friday	Saturday
	1	**2**	**3**	**4**	**5**	**6** New Moon
7	**8**	**9**	**10**	**11**	**12**	**13**
14	**15**	**16**	**17**	**18**	**19**	**20** Full Moon
21	**22**	**23**	**24**	**25**	**26**	**27**
28	**29**	**30**	**31**			

July 6, 2024, Cancer New Moon 14°23'.

July 20, 2024, Full Moon Capricorn 29°08'.

Best money rituals

July 6, 20 and 22, the Sun enters Leo.

Cleaning to Get Customers.

Crush ten shelled hazelnuts and a sprig of parsley in a mortar and pestle.

Boil two liters of Full Moon water and add the ingredients you crushed. Let it boil for 10 minutes and then strain it.

With this infusion you will clean the floor of your business, from the entrance door to the bottom of it.

You must repeat this cleansing every Monday and Thursday for a month, if possible, at the time of the planet Mercury.

Attracts Material Abundance. Moon in Crescent Quarter

You need:

- 1 gold coin or a gold object, without stones.

- 1 copper coin

- 1 silver coin

During a Crescent Moon night with the coins in your hands, go to a place where the Moon's rays illuminate them.

With your hands raised you will repeat: "Moon, help me so that my fortune always grows, and prosperity always accompanies me".

Make the coins ring inside your hands.

Then you will keep them in your wallet. You can repeat this ritual every month.

Spell to Create an Economic Shield for your Business or work.

You need:
- 5 yellow flower petals
- Sunflower seeds
- Sun-dried lemon peel
- Wheat flour
- 3 coins of common use

Crush the yellow flowers and sunflower seeds in a mortar and pestle, then add the lemon peel and the wheat flour.

Mix the ingredients well and store them together with the three coins in a hermetically sealed jar.

This preparation should be used every morning before leaving home.

You should introduce the fingertips of the five fingers of your left hand first and then of your right hand into the bottle, then rub it on the palms of your hands.

Best Rituals for Love

Any day in July.

Express Money Spell.

This spell is most effective if you cast it on a Thursday.

You are going to fill a glass bowl with rice.

Then you light a green candle (which you must have previously consecrated) and place it in the center of the fountain.

You light the cinnamon incense and circle the fountain with its smoke clockwise six times.

While performing this procedure, mentally repeat: "I open my mind and heart to wealth.

Abundance comes to me, now and all is well.

The universe is radiating wealth into my life, now". The leftovers you can throw away in the trash.

Bathroom to Attract Financial Gain

You need:

- 1 rue plant

- Flowery water

- 5 yellow flowers

- 5 tablespoons of honey

- 5 cinnamon sticks

- 5 drops of sandalwood essence

- 1 stick of sandalwood incense

On the first day of the Crescent Moon during an hour favorable for prosperity, boil all the ingredients for five minutes, except for the Agua Florida and the incense. Divide this bath because you must do it for five days. The one you do not use should be kept cold. Add some Agua Florida to the preparation and light the incense. Take a bath and rinse as usual. Slowly drop the preparation from your neck to your feet. Do this for five consecutive days.

Best Rituals for Health

Any day in July.

Spell for Chronic Pain.

Necessary Elements:

-1 golden candle

-1 white candle

-1 green candle

-1 Black tourmaline

-1 photo of yourself or personal object

-1 glass of Luna water

-Photograph of the person or personal object

Place the 3 candles in a triangle shape and in the center place the photo or personal object. Place the glass of moon water on top of the photo and pour the tourmaline inside. Then you light the candles and repeat the following incantation: "I light this candle to achieve my recovery, invoking my inner fires and the protective salamanders and undines, to transmute this pain and discomfort into healing energy of health and wellness. Repeat this prayer 3 times. When you finish the prayer, take the glass, take out the tourmaline and pour the water into a drain of the house, extinguish the candles with your fingers and keep them to repeat this spell until you fully recover. The tourmaline can be used as an amulet for health.

Immediate Improvement Spell

You must get a white candle, a green candle, and a yellow candle. You will consecrate them (from the base to the wick) with pine essence and place them on a table with a light blue tablecloth, in the shape of a triangle. In the center, place a small glass container with alcohol and a small amethyst. At the base of the container a piece of paper with the name of the sick person or a photo with his/her full name on the back and date of birth. Light the three candles and leave them burning until they are completely consumed. While performing this ritual visualize the person completely healthy.

Rituals for the Month of August

August 2024

Sunday	**Monday**	**Tuesday**	**Wednesday**	**Thursday**	**Friday**	**Saturday**
				1	**2**	**3**
4 New Moon	**5**	**6**	**7**	**8**	**9**	**10**
11	**12**	**13**	**14**	**15**	**16**	**17**
18 Full Moon	**19**	**20**	**21**	**22**	**23**	**24**
25	**26**	**27**	**28**	**29**	**30**	**31**

August 4, 2024, New Moon Leo 12°33'.

August 18, 2024, Full Moon Aquarius 27°14'.

August 4,5, 2024

Magic Mirror for Money. Full Moon

Get a mirror 40 to 50 cm in diameter and paint the frame black. Wash the mirror with holy water and cover it with a black cloth.

On the first night of the Full Moon expose it to the Moon's rays so that you can see the entire lunar disk in the mirror. Ask the moon to consecrate this mirror to illuminate your desires.

The next Full Moon night draw with a lip crayon the money symbol 7 times ($$$$$$$).

Close your eyes and visualize yourself with all the material abundance you desire. Leave the symbols drawn until the next morning.

Then you clean the mirror until there are no traces of the paint you have used, using holy water. Put your mirror back in a place where no one will touch it.

You must recharge the energy of the mirror three times a year with Full Moons to repeat the spell.

If you do this on a planetary hour that has to do with prosperity, you will be adding super energy to your intention.

Ritual to Accelerate Sales. New Moon

This is an effective recipe for the protection of money, the multiplication of sales in your business and the energetic healing of the place.

You need:

-1 green candle
-1 coin
- sea salt
-1 pinch of hot pepper

You should perform this ritual on a Thursday or Sunday at the time of the planet Jupiter or the Sun.

There should be no other persons on the business premises.

Light the candle and around it, in the shape of a triangle, place the coin, a handful of salt and a pinch of hot pepper.

It is essential that you place the pepper on the right and the handful of salt on the left. The coin should be at the top of the pyramid.

Stay for a few minutes in front of the candle and visualize everything you are wishing for regarding prosperity.

The remains can be thrown away, the coin is kept in your place of business for protection.

Best Rituals for Love

Any Friday, the day of Venus.

Best Rituals for Love

July 7,14, 21,28, 31.

Spell to Make Someone Think of You

Get a small mirror that we women use for makeup and place a picture of yourself behind the mirror.

Then you take a photograph of the person you want to think about you and place it face down in front of the mirror (so that the two photos are facing each other with the mirror between them).

Wrap the mirror with a piece of red cloth and tie it with a red thread so that they are secure, and the photographs cannot move.

This should be placed under your bed well hidden.

Spell to Become a Magnet

To have a magnetic aura and attract people, you must make a yellow bag containing the heart of a white dove and the eyes of a powdered turtle.

This pouch should be carried in your right pocket if you are a man.

Women will wear this same pouch, but inside the bra on the left side.

Best Rituals for Health

August 23, the Sun enters Virgo.

Ritual Bath with Bitter Herbs

This ritual is used when the person has been so powerfully bewitched that his or her life is in danger.

Necessary Elements:

- *7 Myrtle leaves*
- *Pomegranate juice*
- *Goat milk*
- *Sea salt*
- *Sacred water*
- *Husk*
- *8 Leaves of the wall-breaking plant*

Pour the goat's milk in a large container, add the pomegranate juice, sacred water, plants, sea salt and cascarilla.

Leave this preparation for three hours in front of a white candle and then pour it on your head. You should sleep like this and the next day rinse.

Rituals for the Month of September

September 2024

Sunday	Monday	Tuesday	Wednesday	Thursday	Friday	Saturday
1	**2**	**3** New Moon	**4**	**5**	**6**	**7**
8	**9**	**10**	**11**	**12**	**13**	**14**
15	**16**	**17** Full Moon	**18**	**19**	**20**	**21**
22	**23**	**24**	**25**	**26**	**27**	**28**
29	**30**					

September 3, 2024, Virgo New Moon 11°03'.

September 17, 2024, Full Moon, and Pisces Partial Eclipse 25°40'

Best money rituals

September 3,13,20,2024

Ritual to Get Money in Three Days.

Get five cinnamon sticks, a dried orange peel, a liter of Full Moon water and a silver candle. Boil the cinnamon and orange peel in the Moon water. When it cools place it in a spray bottle. Light the candle in the north part of the living room of your house and spray all the rooms with the liquid. As you do this repeat in your mind: "Spirit Guides protect my home and let me receive the money I need immediately".

When you finish, leave the candle burning.

Money with a White Elephant

Buy a white elephant with the trunk facing up.

Place it facing the interior of your home or business, never in front of the doors.

On the first day of each month, place a bill of the lowest value in the elephant's trunk, folded in two lengthwise and repeat: "May this be doubled by 100";

then fold it again widthwise and repeat: "May this be multiplied by a thousand".

Unfold the bill and leave it in the elephant's trunk until the next month.

Repeat the ritual, changing banknotes.

Lottery Winning Ritual.

You need:
- *2 green candles*
- *12 coins (representing the twelve months of the year)*
- *1 tangerine*
- *Cinnamon stick*
- *Petals of 2 red roses*
- *1 wide-mouth glass jar with a lid*
- *1 old lottery ticket*
- *Full Moon Water*

In the jar place the tangerine, around it the lottery ticket, the coins, the petals, and the cinnamon, cover it with the Moon water and cover it. On the lid of the jar place the candle and light it. The next day you will replace the candle with a new one and on the third day you will uncover the container, throw away everything except the coins, which will serve as an amulet. Keep one in your wallet and leave the other eleven at home. At the end of the year, you must spend the coins.

Best Rituals for Love

Any Friday in September 2024

Ritual to Eliminate Arguments

You should write on a piece of paper the full names of you and your partner. You place it under a pyramid of rose quartz and repeat in your mind: "I (your name) am in peace and harmony with my partner (your partner's name), love surrounds us now and always".

This pyramid with the names should be kept in the love zone of your home. The bottom right corner from the front door is the zone of couples, love, marriage, or relationships.

Ritual to be reciprocated in love.

For a period of five days and at the same time you should make a pyramid on the floor with red rose petals. In a green candle you print the name of the person you want to love, light it, and place it in the center of the pyramid, above the pentacle #3 of Venus.

You sit in front of this pyramid and repeat mentally: "I invoke all the elemental forces of the universe so that (name of the person) corresponds to my love". After this time, you can throw away the remains of the candles in the trash and burn the pentacle.

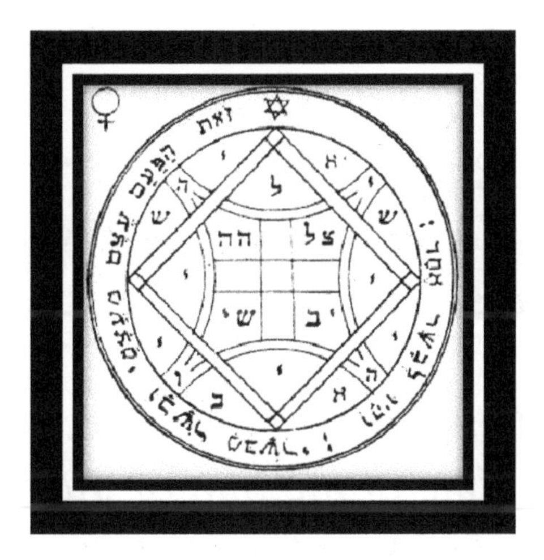

Pentacle # 3 Venus.

Best Rituals for Health

Any day in September. Preferably Monday and Friday.

Healing Bath

Necessary elements:

- *Eggplant*
- *Sage*
- *Ruda*
- *Aguardiente*
- *Husk*
- *Florida Water*
- *Rainwater*
- *Green Candle (if it is in pyramidal form, more effective)*

This bath is more effective if you do it on a Sunday at the time of the Sun or Jupiter. Cut the eggplant into small pieces and place it in a large pot.

Then boil the sage and rue in the rainwater. Strain the liquid over the pieces of eggplant, add the Agua Florida, the brandy, the cascarilla, and light the candle. Pour the mixture into the water for your bath. If you do not have a bathtub, you pour it on top and you dry yourself with the air, you do not use the towel.

Protective Bath before Surgical Operation

Necessary elements:

- *Purple Bell*
- *Coconut Water*
- *Husk*
- *Cologne 1800*
- *Always Alive*
- *Mint Leaves*
- *Rue leaves*
- *Rosemary Leaves*
- *White Candle*
- *Lavender Oil*

This bath is most effective if you do it on a Thursday at the time of the Moon or Mars.

You boil all the plants in the coconut water, when it cools you strain it and add the husk, cologne, lavender oil and light the candle in the west part of your bathroom.

Pour the mixture into the bath water. If you do not have a bathtub, pour it over yourself and do not dry yourself.

Rituals for the Month of October

October 2024

Sunday	Monday	Tuesday	Wednesday	Thursday	Friday	Saturday
		1	**2** New Moon	**3**	**4**	**5**
6	**7**	**8**	**9**	**10**	**11**	**12**
13	**14**	**15**	**16** Full Moon	**17**	**18**	**19**
20	**21**	**22**	**23**	**24**	**25**	**26**
27	**28**	**29**	**30**	**31**		

October 2, 2024, Annular Solar Eclipse in Libra, and New Moon 10°02'.

October 16, 2024, Aries Full Moon 24°34

Best money rituals

October 2, 17, 31, 2024.

Spell with Sugar and Seawater for Prosperity.

You need:
- Seawater
- 3 tablespoons sugar
- 1 cobalt glass cup

Fill the cup with sea water and the sugar, leave it outdoors the first night of the Full Moon and remove it from the serene at 6:00 am.

Then you open the doors of your house and start sprinkling the sugar water from the entrance to the bottom, use a spray bottle, while you do it you must repeat in your mind: "I attract to my life all the prosperity and wealth that the universe knows I deserve, thank you, thank you, thank you".

La Canela

It is used to purify the body. In certain cultures, it is believed that its power consists in helping to immortality. From a magical point of view, cinnamon is linked to the power of the moon because of its feminine tendency.

Ritual to Attract Money Instantly.

You need:
- 5 cinnamon sticks
- 1 dried orange peel
- 1 liter of sacred water
- 1 green candle

Bring the cinnamon, orange peel and liter of water to a boil, then let the mixture stand until it cools. Pour the liquid into a spray bottle.

Light the candle in the north part of the living room of your house and sprinkle all the rooms while repeating: "Angel of Abundance I invoke your presence in this house so that nothing is lacking, and we always have more than we need".

When you finish, give thanks three times, and leave the candle burning.

You can do it on a Sunday or Thursday at the time of the planet Venus or Jupiter.

Best Rituals for Love

Any day in October 2024.

Spell to Forget an Old Love

You need:
- *3 yellow pyramid-shaped candles*
- *Sea salt*
- *White vinegar*
- *Olive oil*
- *Yellow paper*
- *1 black sachet*

This ritual is most effective if you perform it during the phase of the Waning Moon.

You will write in the center of the paper the name of the person you wish to get away from your life with the olive oil.

Then you place the candles on top of it in the shape of a pyramid.

While performing this operation repeat in your mind: "My guardian angel takes care of my life, this is my wish, and it will come true".

When the candles are consumed you will wrap all the remains in the same paper and sprinkle it with the vinegar.

Then place it in the black bag and throw it in a place away from your house, preferably with trees.

Spell to Attract your Soul Mate

You need:

- *Rosemary leaves*
- *Parsley leaves*
- *Basil leaves*
- *Metal container*
- *1 red heart-shaped candle*
- *Cinnamon essential oil*
- *1 heart drawn on red paper*
- *Alcohol*
- *Lavender oil*

You must first consecrate the candle with the cinnamon oil, then light it and place it next to the metal container.

Mix in the container all the plants. Write in the paper heart all the characteristics of the person you want in your life, write the details. Pour five drops of lavender oil on the paper and place it inside the container. Sprinkle it with the alcohol and set it on fire. All the remains should be scattered on the seashore, while you do it, concentrate and ask for that person to come into your life.

Ritual to attract Love.

You need.

- Rose oil
- 1 rose quartz
- 1 apple
- 1 red rose in a small vase
- 1 white rose on a small vase
- 1 long red ribbon
- 1 red candle

For maximum effectiveness, this ritual should be performed on a Friday or Sunday at the time of the planet Venus or Jupiter.

You must consecrate the candle before starting the ritual with rose oil. Light the candle. Cut the apple into two pieces and place one in the red rose vase and the other in the white rose vase. Tie the red ribbon around the two vases. Leave them all night next to the candle until the candle burns out. While you perform this operation repeat in your mind: "May the person who is destined to make me happy appear in my path, I receive and accept it". When the roses are dry, together with the apple halves, bury them in your yard or in a pot with the rose quartz.

Best Rituals for Health

Every Sunday in October 2024

Ritual to Increase Vitality

Soak an aluminum pyramid in a bucket of water for 24 hours. The next day after your regular bath, rinse yourself with this water. You can perform this ritual once a week.

Rituals for the Month of November

November 2024

Sunday	Monday	Tuesday	Wednesday	Thursday	Friday	Saturday
					1 New Moon	**2**
3	**4**	**5**	**6**	**7**	**8**	**9**
10	**11**	**12**	**13**	**14**	**15** Full Moon	**16**
17	**18**	**19**	**20**	**21**	**22**	**23**
24	**25**	**26**	**27**	**28**	**29**	**30** New Moon

November 1, 2024, Scorpio New Moon 9°34'.

November 15, 2024, Full Moon Taurus 24°00'.

November 30, 2024, Sagittarius New Moon 9°32'.

Best money rituals

November 1,15,30, 2024

Make your Stone to Earn Money

You need:

- Earth

- Sacred Water

- 7 coins of any denomination

- 7 pyrite stones

- 1 green candle

- 1 teaspoon cinnamon

- 1 teaspoon sea salt

- 1 teaspoon brown sugar

- 1 teaspoon rice

You must perform this ritual under the light of the full moon, i.e., outdoors.

Inside a container pour the water with the earth so that it becomes a thick mass. Add to the mixture the teaspoons of salt, sugar, rice and cinnamon, and place in various places, in the middle of the dough, the 7 coins and the 7 pyrites. Mix uniformly this mixture, smooth it with a spoon. Leave the container under the light of the full moon all night, and part of the next day in the sun to dry. Once dry, take it inside your house and place the lighted green candle on top of it. Do not clean this stone of the remains of wax. Place it in your kitchen, as close to a window as possible.

Best Rituals for Love
Every Friday and Monday in November.

Magic Mirror of Love

Get a mirror 40 to 50 cm in diameter and paint the frame black. Wash the mirror with sacred water and cover it with a black cloth. On the first night of the Full Moon, you leave it exposed to its rays so that you can see the entire lunar disk in the mirror.

Ask the Moon to consecrate this mirror to illuminate your desires.

The next night of the Full Moon you write with a lip crayon everything you desire concerning love. Specify how you want your partner to be in every way. You close your eyes and visualize yourself happy and with her. You leave the written words until the next morning.

Then you clean the mirror until there are no traces of the paint you have used, using holy water. Put your mirror back in a place where no one will touch it.

You must recharge the mirror three times a year with the energy of the Full Moons to repeat this spell. If you do this on a planetary hour that has to do with love, you will be adding a superpower to your intention.

Passion Enhancement Spell

You need:
- 1 sheet of green paper
- 1 green apple
- Red thread
- 1 knife

This ritual must be performed on a Friday at the hour of the planet Venus.

You write on the green sheet of paper your partner's name and yours and draw a heart around it.

Cut the apple in half with the knife and place the paper between the two halves.

Then tie the halves with the red thread and tie 5 knots.

You are going to take a bite of the apple and swallow that piece.

At midnight you will bury the remains of the apple as close as possible to your partner's house, if you live together, you will bury it in your garden.

Best Rituals for Health

Every Thursday in November 2024

Ritual to Eliminate a pain.

You should lie on your back with your head facing North and place a yellow pyramid on your lower abdomen for 10 minutes, so the ailments will disappear.

Relaxation Ritual

You should take a violet pyramid in your hands and then lie on your back with your eyes closed, keep your mind blank and breathe gently. At that moment you will feel that your arms, legs, and thorax become numb.

Afterwards you will feel them heavier, this means that you are totally relaxed, this ritual generates peace and harmony.

Ritual for a Healthy Old Age

You must take a large egg and paint it gold.

When the paint dries you place it inside a circle that you will make with 7 candles (1 red, 1 yellow, 1 green, 1 pink, 1 blue, 1 purple, 1 white). You sit in front of the circle with your head covered by a white scarf and light the candles clockwise. Repeat the following affirmations as you light them:

I am becoming the best version of myself.
My possibilities are endless.
I have the freedom and power to create the life I want.
I choose to be kind to myself and love myself unconditionally.
I do what I can, and that is enough.
Every day is an opportunity to start over.
Wherever I am on my journey is where I belong.
Let the candles burn out.

Then bury the egg inside a clay pot and fill it with beach sand, leave it exposed to the light of the sun and the moon for three days and three consecutive nights.

You will keep this pot inside your house for three years, at the end of that time you dig up the egg, break the shell and whatever you find inside you will leave it in your house as a protective amulet.

Spell to Cure the Seriously Ill

You must place in a metal container the doctor's diagnosis and a current photo of the person. Place two green candles on either side of it and light them.

Burn the contents of the container and while burning add the person's hair.

When there are only ashes, place them in a green envelope, the sick person should sleep with this envelope under his pillow for 17 days.

Rituals for the Month of December

December 2024

Sunday	Monday	Tuesday	Wednesday	Thursday	Friday	Saturday
1	**2**	**3**	**4**	**5**	**6**	**7**
8	**9**	**10**	**11**	**12**	**13**	**Fourteen** ○ Full Moon
15	**16**	**17**	**18**	**19**	**20**	**21**
22	**23**	**24**	**25**	**26**	**27**	**28**
29	**30** ● New Moon	**31**				

December 15, 2024, Gemini Full Moon 23°52'.

December 30, 2024, Capricorn New Moon 9°43'.

Best money rituals

December 14, 20, 30, 2024

Hindu Ritual to Attract Money.

The perfect days for this ritual are Thursday or Sunday, at the time of the planet Venus, Jupiter, or the Sun.
You need:
- Rue or basil essential oil
- 1 gold coin
- 1 new purse or wallet
- 1 ear of wheat
- 5 pyrites

You must consecrate the golden coin by anointing it with basil or rue oil and dedicating it to Jupiter. While you are anointing it, repeat mentally:

"I want you to saturate this coin with your energy so that economic abundance will come into my life."

Then you put oil on the ear of wheat and offer it to Jupiter asking him not to lack food in your home. You take the coin together with the five pyrites and you place it in the new coin box, you must bury it in the front left side of your house. The ear of corn you will keep it in the kitchen of your house.

Money and Abundance for all Family Members.

You need:
- 4 earthenware containers
- 4 pentacles #7 of Jupiter (you can print them)

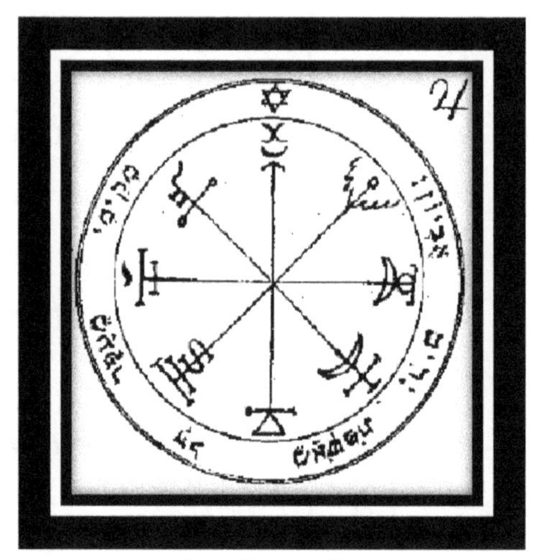

Pentacle #7 of Jupiter.

- Honey
- 4 citrines

On Friday at the hour of the planet Jupiter you print the names of all the people living in your home on the back of the seventh pentacle of Jupiter.

Then place each piece of paper in the clay pots along with the citrines and pour honey on it. Place the pots in the four cardinal points of your home. Leave them there for a month. At the end of this time, you throw away the honey and the pentacles, but you keep the citrines in your living room.

Best daily rituals for Love
Friday and Sunday December 2024

Ritual to Turn a Friendship into Love

This ritual is most powerful if you perform it on a Tuesday at the hour of Venus.

You need:

- *1 Full-length photo of the person you love*
- *1 small mirror*
- *7 of your hair*
- *7 drops of your blood*
- *1 red pyramid candle*
- *1 golden sachet*

Pour the drops of your blood on the mirror, place the hair on top and wait for it to dry. Place the photograph on top of the mirror (when the blood is dry).

You light the candle and place it to the right of the mirror, concentrate and repeat:

"We are united forever by the power of my blood and the power of (name of the person you love) the love I feel for you. Friendship ends, but eternal love begins."

When the candle is consumed you must place it all inside the golden bag and throw it into the sea.

Germanic Love Spell

This spell is most effective if you perform it during the Full Moon phase at 11:59 pm at night.

You need:
- 1 photograph of the person you love
- 1 photograph of you
- 1 White dove heart
- 13 sunflower petals
- 3 pins
- 1 pink candle
- 1 blue candle
- 1 new sewing needle
- Brown sugar
- Cinnamon powder
- 1 table

Place the photographs on top of the board, put the heart on top and stick the three pins in it. Surround them with the sunflower petals and place the pink candle on the left and the blue candle on the right and light them in the same order.

You prick your index finger of your left hand and let three drops of blood fall over your heart. While the blood is falling you repeat three times: "By the power of the blood you (name of the person) belong to me".

When the candles are consumed you bury everything and before closing the hole you put cinnamon powder and brown sugar.

Spell of Vengeance

You need:
- 1 river stone
- Red pepper
- Photograph of the person who stole your love
- 1 pot
- Cemetery soil
- 1 black candle

You must write on the back of the photo the following incantation: "By the power of vengeance I promise you that you will pay me back and never hurt anyone again, you are cancelled.

(Name of person)".

Then place the photo of the person in the bottom of the pot and put the stone on top, pour the cemetery soil and red pepper, in this order.

You light the black candle and repeat the same incantation you wrote behind the photo. When the candle is consumed throw it in the trash and the flowerpot you leave it in a place that is a mountain.

Best Rituals for Health

Any Thursday in December 2024

Crystalline Grill for Health

*The first step is to decide what goal you want to manifest. You will write on a piece of paper your desires in reference to your health, always in the present tense, they should not contain the word **NO.** An example would be "I have perfect health".*

Necessary Elements.

- *1 large amethyst quartz (the focus)*
- *4 Larimar*
- *4 small carnelian quartz*
- *6 tiger eye quartz*

- 4 citrines
- 1 Geometric figure of the Flower of life
- 1 White quartz tip to activate the grid

Flower of Life.

This quartz should be cleaned before the ritual to purify your stones from the energies they may have absorbed before reaching your hands, sea salt is the best option. Leave them with sea salt overnight. When you take them out you can also light a palo santo and smoke them to enhance the purification process.

The geometric patterns help us to better visualize how the energies connect between the nodes; the nodes are the decisive points in the geometry, they are the strategic positions where you will place the crystals, so that their energies interact with each other creating energetic currents of high vibrations, (as if it were a circuit) which we can divert towards our intention.

You will look for a quiet place because when we work with crystalline wefts we are working with universal energies.

You will take the stones one by one and place them in your left hand, which you will have in the form of a bowl, cover it with your right hand and repeat aloud the names of the reiki symbols: Cho Ku Rei, Sei He Ki, Hon Sha Ze Sho Nen and Dai Ko Mio, three consecutive times each.

You will do this to energize your stones.

*Fold your paper and place it in the center of the net. You place the large amethyst quartz on top, this stone in the center is the focus, the others you place as in the *example.*

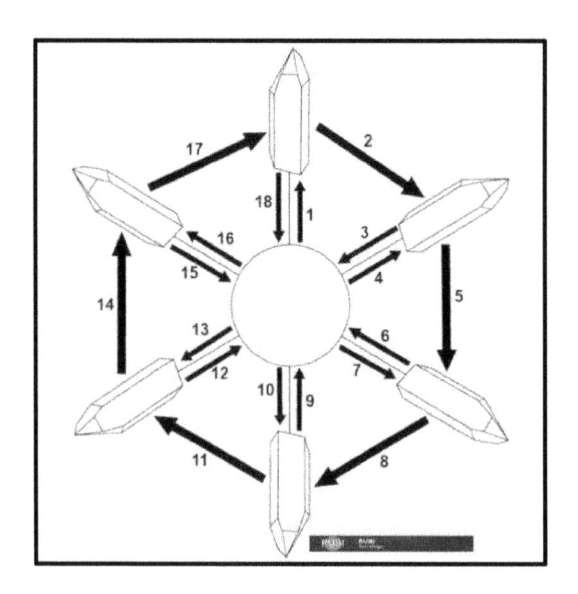

You are going to connect them with the quartz tip, starting with the circular focus in a clockwise direction.

When you have set up the grill leave it in an area where no one can touch it. Every few days you should reconnect it, that is, activate it with the quartz tip, visualizing in your mind what you wrote on the paper.

About the Author

In addition to her astrological knowledge, Alina A. Rubi has an abundant professional education; she holds certifications in Psychology, Hypnosis, Reiki, Bioenergetic Crystal Healing, Angelic Healing, Dream Interpretation and is a Spiritual Instructor. Rubi has knowledge of Gemology, which she uses to program stones or minerals and turn them into powerful Amulets or Talismans of protection.

Rubi has a practical and purposeful character, which has allowed her to have a special and integrative vision of several worlds, facilitating solutions to specific problems. Alina writes the Monthly Horoscopes for the website of the American Association of Astrologers; you can read them at www.astrologers.com. At this moment she writes a weekly column in the newspaper El Nuevo Herald on spiritual topics, published every Sunday in digital form and on Mondays in print. He also has a program and weekly Horoscope on the YouTube channel of this newspaper. Her Astrological Yearbook is published every year in the newspaper "Diario las Américas", under the column Rubi Astrologa.

Rubi has authored several articles on astrology for the monthly publication "Today's Astrologer", has taught classes on Astrology, Tarot, Palm Reading, Crystal Healing, and Esotericism. She has weekly videos on esoteric topics on her YouTube channel: Rubi Astrologa. She had her own Astrology show broadcasted daily through Flamingo T.V., has been interviewed by several T.V. and radio programs, and every year she publishes her "Astrological Yearbook" with the horoscope sign by sign, and other interesting mystical topics.

She is the author of the books "Rice and Beans for the Soul" Part I, II, and III, a compilation of esoteric articles, published in English, Spanish, French, Italian and Portuguese. "Money for All Pockets", "Love for All Hearts", "Health for All Bodies", Astrological Yearbook 2021, Horoscope 2022, Rituals and Spells for Success in 2022, and 2023 Spells and Secrets, Astrology Classes, Rituals and Charms 2024 and Chinese Horoscope 2024 all available in nine languages: English, Russian, Portuguese, Chinese, Italian, French, Spanish, Japanese and German.

Rubi speaks English and Spanish perfectly, combining all her talents and knowledge in her readings. She currently resides in Miami, Florida.

For more information you can ***visit the website*** ***www.esoterismomagia.com***

Angeline A. Rubi is the daughter of Alina Rubi. She is the editor of all the books. She is currently studying psychology at Florida International University. She is the author of "Protein for Your Mind," a collection of metaphysical articles.

Since she was a child, she has been interested in metaphysical and esoteric subjects, and has practiced astrology and Kabbalah since she was four years old. She has knowledge of Tarot, Reiki, and Gemology.

For more information, please contact her by email:
rubiediciones29@gmail.com

Milton Keynes UK
Ingram Content Group UK Ltd.
UKHW030418131223
434231UK00012B/576